Chapter 1

To Lance! Thank you for being the first to buy my book! I love ya!
♡ Emma
   (a.k.a Bronze Chainz)

© 2018 Emma Killian. All Rights Reserved.
ISBN 978-1-387-88929-7

instagram.com/lonelyscatteredpieces

For those who feel like they're stuck in chapter one.

Table of Contents

Mistakes	6
Dreams	7
Fly Away	8
Suicide	9
Loveless	10
Loneliness	11
Storm	12
Letters	13
Beauty	14
Reflexes	15
Shove	16
Never Fully You	17
The Song of Change	18
Promise	19
Tower	20
Greener Grass	21
Fatal Fact	22
Too	23
Anger	24
Make Sense	25
Perception	26
Fall Into Place	27
Race	28
If I Died	29
No Control	30
Rain	31
Forget	32
I Will	33
What Have You Done?	34
Wind	35
Mind Control	36
Damage	37
Can You Find	38
Harder To Live	39

I Am Never Lonely	40
Shadow	41
Distance	42
Alive	43
Rulers	44
Deeper Meaning	45
Dirt	46
"I Promise"	47
Dream:Reality	48
Jealousy	49
On Your Own	50
Give Up	51
Moving On	52
Safety In Lies	53
The Bear	54
Movie	55
Uneven	56
Intelligent Life	58
War	59
Explosion	60
Murder	61
I Wish	62
Linger	63
Black Bird	64

Mistakes

I've done many things before
That I do regret
And even though I try to fix my past
It's still, to me, a threat

They say everyone makes mistakes
But this is a bad situation
How can you get rid of a mistake
If it's become your reputation?

-e.k.

Dreams

Dreams can get left behind
Buried under piles of snow
Dusted over under shelves
And no one knows where they go

Dreams are hidden in your heart
In spaces small as cracks of stones
And I know that you believe
It's hard to reach into those zones

But searching will not help
If you've chosen to be blind
You must be strong, determined
And know that this will take some time

If you leave your dreams in the rain
Over time, they will rust
So remember: you will find your way
If you simply remember to dust

-e.k.

Fly Away

I wish I could fly away
And escape this town
Cause you are air, and in this place
I fear that I might drown

I wish I could fly away
And get out of this place
Because you are somewhere else
And I long for your embrace

I wish I could fly away
And go somewhere brand new
I just hope that wherever it is
That I'm going with you

I wish I could fly away
But humans don't have wings
I'm stuck here and it's so lonely
And, oh God, it stings

-e.k.

Suicide

I've wanted to take my life before
But that I'll never do
Because of this one fear I have
I guess I'll share with you

The reason they're left with open eyes
And that their body is left haunted
As the life drains from them, they think
"This isn't what I really wanted"

-e.k.

Loveless

I thought you were in love
But you felt nothing at all
Yet I wanted to believe it
So I let you let me fall

We may be right next to each other
But we're much further apart
Because I'm closest to the heartbeat
But I'm furthest from the heart

-e.k.

Loneliness

I'll only let you come inside my home
If I believe the words you say
And loneliness knocks at the door
Asking if for the night it can stay

Loneliness has tormented me before
But this time I think I'll be alright
So here I am believing again
It'll only stay for one night

-e.k.

Storm

You know that I'm a storm
But you don't know what I've seen
Life shows all the moments
You don't see on TV screens

I know I'm unpredictable
And you don't understand
How the slightest things can make
A person hurt you like I can

But you haven't seen the damage
That I see on the daily
And haven't felt the pain
That's found a home in my body

I know you don't understand
Why weight makes me break so much thunder
But if you ever did know, then
You would only just still wonder

-e.k.

Letters

I tried to send you letters
But from letters you seemed scared
Because of that I didn't know
Whether or not you still cared

I never got a reply
No letters back because of fear
But I never knew
That you still wanted me here

And now we are strangers
And I do not know what for
Cause if only you had spoken
Then I would've held the door

-e.k.

Beauty

You once told me you didn't believe
That you had any worth
Or that the beauty that you had
Existed underneath the dirt

But your eyes have their own stars
That make the sky itself look dull
There are less galaxies in space
Than there are inside your skull

The mountains inside your mind
Have the most wondrous of peaks
And your freckles are so golden
I swear the sun stole from your cheeks

I still can't put it into words
All the wonders that you hold
So I hope to never hear you say again
That you are not beautiful

-e.k.

Reflexes

If someone glances towards us
We're going to do the same
Even if they've looked away
There is no way we can refrain

But now after saying you loved me
You don't seem to anymore
And what scares me most
Is that I can't really be sure

Even if there is one chance
Loving me is all you've got
I will hide from every sign
Of the chance that you might not

So I never want to look at you
If knowing how you feel is what I lack
Because I'm scared that when I look away
You still will not look back

-e.k.

Shove

She never saw her beauty
And for that, envied the world
And that was too much to handle
For a broken little girl

And as the winter grew much colder
Her brittle bones began to crack
And the feelings held inside them
Poured out and drowned her in the black

But the words you never told her
Could have kept her from the cold
And stopped those brittle bones from breaking
As those brittle bones grew old

You were scared she was too fragile
So you never touched her walls
But that just could have saved her
From the winter's tempting calls

Even if she seemed too feeble
You still should have shoved
Cause maybe all she ever needed
Was to know that she was loved

-e.k.

Never Fully You

It seems as though the truth
Is that you're never fully you
Because some parts you call your own
Came from others you once knew

As you meet new people
You will start to change
Little parts of other people
Will begin to build your name

And sometimes you may notice
When others pick up on something new
That the things they do or say
Seem to have come from you

And sometimes when I see others
Start to collect parts of me
I remember what they took
Wasn't part of who I used to be

So I'll think of it the other way
That the people I've become
Each different piece of them
Came from a different someone

It's amazing just to think
That the new parts of me I get
Come from so many people
That I've never even met

-e.k.

The Song of Change

Change will sing a song
That no one else has dared to sing
For they all are scared
Of differences that it will bring

So because of what I'd seen
I kept my mouth shut, too
I didn't want anything to change
All the things in which I knew

But once the world went still
Like the wind and the air
I soon stopped noticing
That the world was even there

And I felt like I was stuck
Ending up in the same place
Like there was no way to break free
From this always losing chase

So I laced up my shoes
And started running down the track
But this time I promised myself
That I would never go back

So even if nobody can
Stand the sounds of change's song
What comes from singing will be worth it
So it's time I sing along

-e.k.

Promise

I once told you I'd be here
Until the very end
That you could always find me
If you needed a friend

I meant it more than anything
That I loved you most
And you'd think I'd take it back
If I knew what I now know

Because now I don't feel anything
My love has seemed to die
And if you knew I know you'd fear
That I would leave your side

But no matter what I feel
I'll stay until I do not wake
Because I once made a promise
And a promise I won't break

-e.k.

Tower

Trapped inside this tower
How much longer can it be
Till someone comes to save you
And finally set you free?

They told you they'd be coming
But all you ever are's alone
So you start to lose your hope
Inside this tower made of stone

And some will come along
That will always let you down
For when they say they're coming
Then they're nowhere to be found

And sometimes it seems better
Now to jump and end it all
Rather than wait for someone
To catch you when you take the fall

But even though it seems being
Alone forever is your fate
You will get out of the tower
If you find the strength to wait

-e.k.

Greener Grass

You looked to find a way
To make your grass green as can be
And upon all of your searching
You happened to find me

The green I showed was blinding
And you wanted yours as bright
You hid all of your intentions
So I would let you inside

But since I never knew you wanted
Only the garden that I grew
I put so many secrets
And so much trust right into you

And as you learned the truth
Of what I'm really all about
The grass started to die
And to grow began your doubt

Now you've learned all about me
Every secret that I hide
You see, my grass was really grey
And every blade of it was dyed

You went to search for a new garden
And told me you'd be right back
So I sat down and I waited
As the blue sky turned to black

All I needed was goodbye
To get me off the ground
But I slowly turned to grey
Because you never came around

-e.k.

Fatal Fact

Your love was never there
Or at least I couldn't see
I told myself that it would surface
If I waited patiently

I told myself you loved me
Cause I needed it to be true
But soon enough, I couldn't run
From the fatal fact I knew

Your ticket left the scanner
You were soon to leave the ground
I told you that I loved you
And you didn't turn around

And then I learned the truth
Your love is what I lack
Not even fighting tears, I left
And I did not look back

-e.k.

Too

I hate to fall in love
Because you will always come first
But you only seem to want me here
Because I boost your worth

I hate to fall in love
Cause when I send you paragraphs
Telling you how much I love you
You never say anything back

I hate to fall in love
Because I've made myself your home
But every time I really need you
I remember I'm alone

I never want to fall in love
Cause I'm certain only one thing is true
"I love you" will never leave your lips
Unless it ends with the word "too"

-e.k.

Anger

The things that I have done
And the things that I have said
Show the truth of who I am
And what's really in my head

And all of these words
That I try so hard to hide
Will eventually come out
When there's no more room inside

These feelings spark a match
And it's me holding the flame
Now I've poured it onto everything
And chose others to blame

Now I've killed everyone
But can't stop what I'm about
Because you cannot tame a fire
If it's all you're breathing out

-e.k.

Make Sense

We all overthink
And define everything we own
And when we get lonely
We ask why we're always alone

When we become hurt
We ask too many questions to count
We all think we can add up
Our answers to an amount

But our questions won't be answered
Cause the answers don't exist
So why spend your life in wonder
When what we know is all there is?

I know life gets so hard
When not knowing is too intense
But I promise, things will be much easier
If you don't try to make sense

-e.k.

Perception

You thought you knew everything
About this inch-deep lake
Everything that lay inside
And how much water it could take

You think that everything you see
Is everything that's true
But how would it feel to know
That there's much more than you knew?

Thought a reflection was the bottom
So you jumped in with both feet
But once your feet touched no ground
You learned what your eyes could truly meet

You'll only ever be so wise
To know there's more than what you thought
And never let your eyes tell you
What is there and what is not

-e.k.

Fall Into Place

The world will let you down
And some things will not make sense
You'll think that things won't ever fit
When everything gets too intense

But maybe there's a world
That is right below your feet
And up here is so much worse
Than everything that lies beneath

And when you think the world
Is trying to beat down on you
Maybe it's just trying to throw you
Hard enough that you'll break through

It's okay to fall
You'll receive nothing more than scrapes
You just need to trip a few more times
For it all to fall into place

-e.k.

Race

We run to beat the race
Everyone trying to win
A common goal to reach the top
And find the place it all begins

But you can't even learn
All that happens while you're alive
So how could you know everything
When so little is archived?

The truth is that nobody
Really knows which way to run
And they don't seem to realize
That this race cannot be won

So I just want you to know
When you think you've seen it all
The only truth in this moment
Is no one's ever been so small

-e.k.

If I Died

Sometimes I wonder if I died
Then how would you feel?
Would your heart turn inside out
But could you keep it all concealed?

Would you realize what you wanted
Is now what you lack?
Would you spend years wishing
You could go and take it back?

But I guess there is no point
To think of the end of my days
Because I know even then
You wouldn't choose me anyways

-e.k.

No Control

If I lost one sense
It wouldn't be so bad
Cause I could find the truth
With the four senses I still had

But what about the times
When they all think I'm insane
It's the most terrifying thing
When I come back into my brain

Cause if you've lost all senses
Each one from one to five
You can't tell what's real, what's not
Or if you're even still alive

-e.k.

Rain

Flowers don't like the rain
When it gives more than they need
For when the rain drenches their soil
All the petals do is plead

They don't think they will survive
But someday the rain will end
And all flowers will bloom
Just as beautiful again

So every time you see
Wet flowers hanging in your view
Remember they'll survive the rain
So you can survive it, too

-e.k.

Forget

I grew myself a forest
And I'll name this one "my mind"
And if you were to walk through
You would wish that you were blind

The memories will wander
Down their paths and through the trees
And some will taint the areas
That their life disagrees

But there's some I can't handle
So I'll grow my vines fast
Have them tangle over everything
I cannot bear to last

Some, though, cannot get
All the way to what I seek
Without covering certain memories
I desperately want to keep

So I'll send out the vines
Which I can't let myself regret
Because I accept this fate
If this is what it takes to forget

-e.k.

I Will

Don't listen to my promise
Cause when you start to fall apart
I won't have the words to help you
I will only break your heart

Don't ever ask me for
Help when you have lost your way
For when you hand me your problems
Sorry's all I'll have to say

Don't listen when I tell you
I will always be here
Because when you really need me
I will only disappear

Please don't depend on me
For when I become your ground
You will always lose your balance
I will only let you down

-e.k.

What Have You Done?

She hears a simple word
And her heart adds another beat
Is this the feeling of anger
Or the feeling of defeat?

Does she have the strength to lie
And tell them that she feels okay?
She knows that she can do it
If she looks the other way

Her eyes begin to swell
And her mind begs to be dead
But she can only seem to focus
On these feelings in her head

She starts to see a face
As she feels herself choke
They tell me no one else is there
But it's your hands around my throat

-e.k.

Wind

She asks the wind a question
And she begs the wind to spill
But she realizes her answer
Once she feels the air go still

-e.k.

Mind Control

You seem to have a power
That no human can obtain
You have found a way
To take control over my brain

Cause if not, what can explain
For hours laying in my bed
I have no other thoughts
Except for you inside my head

-e.k.

Damage

I am so sorry
For all the hurt I have caused you
You don't deserve what I have done
And don't deserve what I will do

I am so sorry
So much damage I can't fix
Yet you still fail to see
That in me, destruction's all there is

Since I cannot fix this
I will leave here in a hearse
It's best to leave without a word
Than to make this any worse

-e.k.

Can You Find

Can you find any happiness
Inside the point you break?
Can you find any hope
In the motivation you fake?

Can you find strength to face the day
When you feel you weigh a ton?
Can you find a reason
When there really isn't one?

-e.k.

Harder To Live

It's harder to live
Not when you're filled with pain
But when every single thing
That you see all looks the same

It's when nothing whispers to you
"You can make it through the day"
When you sit in rooms for hours
But you have nothing to say

When you stare at your ceiling
No clue how much time has gone by
Everything's become so dull
That why you're here you'll wonder why

It's the hardest to live
When the grey spreads to your heart
And it's become all the same shade
You cannot tell the greys apart

-e.k.

I Am Never Lonely

I am never lonely
When I'm on my own at home
Cause that isn't loneliness
That's only being alone

I am never lonely
When it's only you and me
I am not alone
With one person's company

Consider me lonely
In a city or a crowd
In rooms full of people
When their voices get too loud

I've never been so lonely
When there's no one there but me
As I have when everyone's backs
Are the only thing I see

-e.k.

Shadow

All alone, I should've known
That this would be my fate
For all that you are
Is the shadow I create

When I'm in the light
You are always on the ground
But when I'm left in the dark
You are nowhere to be found

-e.k.

Distance

For now I kept my distance
So you would not get sick of me
Since I tend to burn out fast
I had to treat you carefully

And I knew if I came back
It'd be too much and you would leave
But if I stay away too long
You'll soon forget about me

I guess it was always meant to happen
For us to come to an end
Cause I'd rather you be happy
Than remember who I am

-e.k.

Alive

You feel you are above
Anything that can be touched
The world is in slow motion
But your heart is in a rush

In this moment, not a thing
That you own can be lost
And nothing that you do
Could charge you such a cost

When your body feels
Like it is nothing more than air
But at the exact same time
It feels like it's completely there

It is in these moments
That you're furthest from your death
For you are most alive
When you can feel your every breath

-e.k.

Rulers

You and I ruled a kingdom
That lay by the ocean side
Where we would play all day
Above the ocean's changing tide

Years and years go by
Memories start getting lost
And your imagination fades
At an educational cost

There was so much in the world
When we had the time to play
But now that life's become so busy
Everything has turned to grey

We once had ruled the ocean
But now we rarely talk
And now I'm visiting our kingdom
But all I see is rock

-e.k.

Deeper Meaning

Some things may seem boring
No matter how complex or "grand"
Cause people don't enjoy the things
That they cannot understand

-e.k.

Dirt

I once read a poem
Where somebody had told
That every flower had to grow through dirt
To become beautiful

And then they had added
They believed they were no seed
They were only the dirt
In which the flowers were conceived

But if we didn't have others
To help us through hard times
Would we ever make it to
Our long lost finish lines?

So if all you think you are is dirt
It's important that you know
That without you there is nowhere
For any seed to grow

-e.k.

"I Promise"

You can't know the truth behind a promise
So it's up to you to decide
If the action's really worth
That "I promise" could be a lie

-e.k.

Dream:Reality

Why do all our dreams
Always appear so very real?
Why can't we hide them from our memory
When we don't want to feel?

And why do when we want
To keep them, we forget
And when we want them to disappear
They will never leave your head?

I wish that your kiss
Hadn't felt so real and true
Because now it hurts much more
That I will never have you

I wish dreams seemed as real
As staring at a screen
Cause now it feels like we had something
And I just lost it all again

-e.k.

Jealousy

Jealousy destroys you
And they say you mustn't be
But how do I change
If I can't control how I feel?

I try to keep it all together
But I'm not an architect
And because of all the cracks
My feet are starting to get wet

I could float above the water
If I knew how to let go
But how to take my hands off the wheel
Is impossible to know

So I'm sorry to those
Who wait for me on the ground
But I will not make it home
Because this ship is going down

-e.k.

On Your Own

It isn't that other people
Tell you what's wrong and what's right
It's that you're left on your own
Not knowing how you will survive

So you follow other people
Hoping that you won't get lost
But your naive, shallow roots
Will shrivel up when comes the frost

But even if you don't know
What to do or where to go
You'll learn you'll find yourself
In all the places you don't know

So dig your roots in deeper
Find your way all on your own
Cause if you follow behind others
You'll only find yourself alone

I hope one day you'll see
The only one in control is you
Cause when you do things for yourself
You'll learn there's much more you can do

-e.k.

Give Up

Right now, you're alive
If you are reading this
And you must come to see
How beautiful that truly is

I know that you are tired
And you've given all you can
But no one else seems to think
You've put any effort in

But if you keep on going
It's okay to fall apart
And trust me, it will get better
Don't let it end before it starts

I know sometimes it seems
Like it won't ever be enough
But if you're reading this, remember
You've never truly given up

-e.k.

Moving On

Because I have so much
You can say I have it all
But with only one piece missing
Then I'm not really whole

Things tend to get lost
When they make no effort to stay
And things that do not matter
Will always get in the way

And I have lost the only thing
I cannot live without
I want to say it played a smaller part
But it's what my story's all about

They say the only way
To strength is to move on
And if that's my only option
Then I never will be strong

-e.k.

Safety In Lies

Why do we lie
To protect how we feel?
For others will still notice
What we try to keep concealed

Can we stop saying we're alright
When we've yet to let go?
Can we stop saying we forget
When the truth is we don't know?

But if you just admit the truth
You will find you can be strong
And it doesn't matter
If every now and then you're wrong

It's time to let your sadness
And your shame come to a halt
Because the way you made it here
Is in no way your fault

-e.k.

The Bear

A young girl's teddy bear
She had called it her best friend
She told him she would love him
Until the very end

But years and years go by
And she has no time for toys
Without a single thought, she gives it
To her neighbor's little boys

Though the boys said they loved him
They were selfish with no heart
They fought over him till one day
He was nearly torn apart

They thought the bear was useless
Because of its new looks
Then they threw it out
When given brand new story books

Another girl found this frayed bear
Said she'd love it till she'd die
Couldn't hear as she dragged it
When the bear began to cry

And someday she'll toss it out
Just like every other "friend"
And won't care to know the history
Of where this bear has been

-e.k.

Movie

The actors in this move
Don't know that they play a part
But they have been present
Every moment since the start

The setting always changes
And some leave before it ends
But others know for certain
This is right where it begins

Some scenes are far too boring
Some important ones not shown
But it's better they don't see you
When it's just you all alone

But you must learn to love this movie
Fall in love with every piece
If you live life to the fullest
You'll never truly be deceased

Music may keep the movie rolling
Save it when you almost break
But I hope the soundtrack to your life
Sounds more like every breath you take

-e.k.

Uneven, Part I

She wakes up on a mattress
Strewn across the dirty floor
Doesn't think she has the strength
To even make it to her door

She doesn't change, for she
Only has two pairs of clothes
Living on her own
Aching from her head to her toes

She's not surprised to find
That she has nothing to eat
She hopes there'll be something cheap enough
At the market down the street

She opens her door to find
That the sky has fallen down
And tries hard to ignore the pieces
Strewn across the heavy ground

But no matter what she does
She feels the shards cut up her feet
So she sat before she could
Even make it to the street

Then she saw a little girl
Who was also staring back
She wondered what it would be like
To have everything she had

As she felt a tear slip down her face
She held a shard of a broken cloud
And she couldn't even feel
A drop of blood fall to the ground

Uneven, Part II

She wakes up in her bed
That could easily fit four
But she has it all to herself
And still hopes of having more

After she takes a shower
She picks a pair of clothes
From her walk-in closet
And the hundred outfits that she owns

She eats her yummy breakfast
That her mother had made up
And throws the rest of it away
When she feels she's had enough

She bursts out the door
Running down the street to shop
Looking in the windows
For something to make her stop

But nothing catches her eye
So she goes to turn around
But spots a sad-looking girl
Sitting alone on the ground

She wonders why she's upset
Was she banned from her phone's use?
Did her parents tell her no
When she asked for something new?

But she just ignored the girl
When the girl began to cry
And just kept walking on
Under a blue, unbroken sky

-e.k.

Intelligent Life

The world is so full
Of sad people and frowns
But I bet you that'd change
If they all looked around

Realized how lucky we are
To live on this earth
To have obsessions and people
That give us our worth

To be able to understand
To learn and be smart
To have our emotions
And to follow our heart

To have them broken
For reasons we don't know
But to learn to be strong
And to learn to let go

To love what we have
Even when we receive
And to learn to move on
Every time we must leave

How lucky to be aware
To build up our lists
And know there's so much out there
We've not seen that exists

-e.k.

War

Do you think it's possible
For all the pain to end?
For the fights to become silent?
For enemies to make amends?

Well you must be naive
To believe love can end this mess
Cause such a weapon won't affect
The stone-cold hearts of the ruthless

The only way to freedom
Is through violence and through war
Even when it seems
Like we've lost track of any score

Cause the greedy won't stop chasing
Predator after innocent prey
And they'll keep going after
All the red just looks like grey

-e.k.

Explosion

I can feel heat from the fire
And the trembling of the ground
But it wasn't loud enough
To hide my ears from the sound

Of the people screaming
As the rocks falls from the sky
Resonating as an echo
Of each person's piercing cry

I know that this is my fault
But I wish it wasn't true
That I have done more damage
Than this bomb could ever do

I wish I could go back
And melt away into the ash
Because I'm the only person
Who had left without a scratch

-e.k.

Murder

When I regain consciousness
I am horrified to find
Blood covering my hands
That grip tightly to a knife

I want to believe
That in this darkness, I'm alone
But the truth is that I know
That this blood is not my own

Frozen still with fear
I slowly shift my eyes down
And find a silhouette
Lying still on the ground

Suddenly I'm by his side
Searching for a pulse or breath
But the cold of his skin
Tells me he has met his death

I killed somebody innocent
Who did not deserve this
And will cause those he knew
A lifetime of unhappiness

I start to go insane
Losing sense of where I am
But I need to remember
That this is how this all began

So I want to be sorry
But I must stay sane instead
And the only way is to believe
Somebody else wanted you dead

-e.k.

I Wish

I wish that you would stop
And find me when you felt
Like your world was coming down
And you couldn't save yourself

I wish I'd be the person
That you would come to first
Who, instead of causing it,
Would take away your hurt

I wish when you were lonely
I would be the one you'd call
Always there to remind you
Why you breathe the air at all

But you will not stop
And you're fine all on your own
But I'll never stop wishing
That I wasn't so alone

-e.k.

Linger

I have always wondered
Why when people cut their ties
They say the past goes down the drain
And all that they've built dies

Just because it is no longer
Doesn't mean it wasn't there
It will always walk beside you
And will linger in the air

And you will learn something new
From every choice you make
So no matter what it was
It was never a mistake

And everything you go through
Works so hard to make you strong
So if you think good only comes from stillness
You should know that you are wrong

-e.k.

Black Bird

Everything around stood still
As she waited patiently
Till she saw a black bird flying
Fast over every grey tree

In a moment, it was gone
All went back to its still state
She hoped she'd see more movement
And she continued to wait

But after years of waiting
She decided to walk home
Nothing, to her, had changed
As she watched the planet grow

And she wondered yet again
If the gears would ever turn
Would a spark ever appear
To make the fire inside burn?

So when she returned home
At the start of a long night
She tried to fall asleep
In hopes it would speed up her life

But when the black bird hit the window
She was woken by the sound
And when she went to see what happened
She saw the bird dead on the ground

But when it flew fast through the sky
It had blocked out all the light
For she noticed all its feathers
Were the brightest shade of white

-e.k.